relief and design transfer

relief and design transfer:
creating a three-dimensional illusion on a flat surface

(previously published as *Transfer: Designs, Textures and Images*)

harold stevens

Associate Professor of Art
C. W. Post College, Long Island University

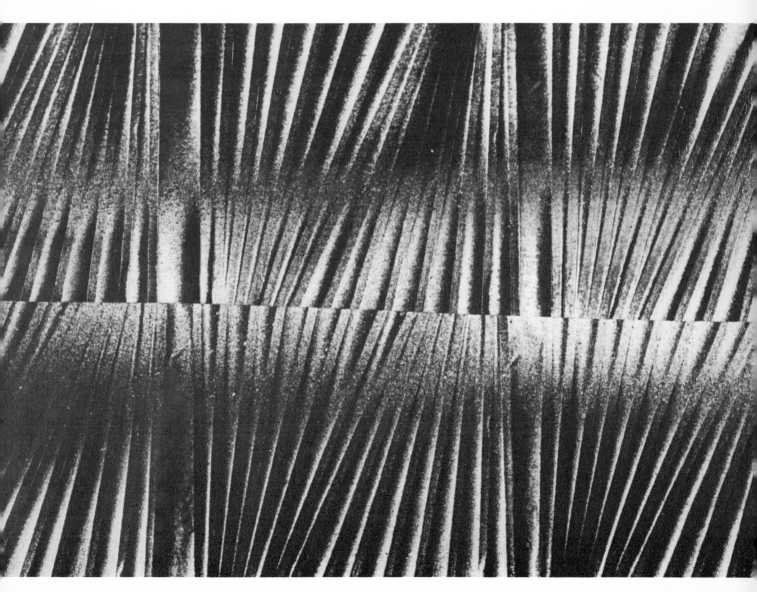

HAWTHORN BOOKS, INC.
PUBLISHERS / NEW YORK

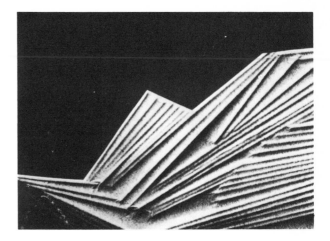

Library of Congress Catalog Card Number: 75-28702
ISBN: 0–8015–6277–5

1 2 3 4 5 6 7 8 9 10

Published by arrangement with Davis Publications, Inc.

contents

acknowledgments

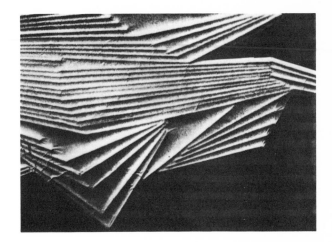

During the years of experimentation with *the relief transfer* process, I frequently found myself in need of advice, information, and encouragement. On these occasions I turned to a fellow artist, Harry Hoehn, a master printmaker who is the inventor of a new planographic printing process called "dry lithography". He helped me in countless ways, not the least of which was suggesting the very appropriate name, "relief transfer". I am deeply grateful to him for all that he has done.

I also wish to thank two young women, Ellen Robbins and Julia Sanchez, for providing the skillful hands that appear in many of the photographs.

Finally, my thanks to Davis Publications for making this book possible.

The Author

introduction

The purpose of this book is to introduce the reader to the transfer processes and the techniques required to transfer images from one surface to another. A number of the more popular processes—decalcomania, rubbings, monoprinting, and others—are covered in sufficient depth to introduce the beginner to these interesting design processes and to stimulate further experimentation by those familiar with these techniques.

The emphasis of this book, however, is the versatile and fascinating process of relief transfer—a method of translating a three-dimensional surface into a two-dimensional representation of that surface. An understanding of the many traditional techniques adds to the variations possible in relief transfer. It can convert the bark of a tree, for example, into a flat design that retains all of the detailed texture of bark. It is similar to rubbing, in certain respects, but it goes much further in its ability to recreate with the clarity of a photograph the actual three-dimensional appearance of a surface.

It is essentially a painting technique but it can be applied to printmaking and collage as well. Which-ever way it is used, it can provide the artist with a fresh and dramatic approach to the handling of light and color and to the realization of highly expressive imagery and design.

For the student it offers opportunities for endless exploration and discovery in a whole new world of exciting texture, color, and form. It also provides, for those with some experience and training, a way of getting results that are difficult to obtain with traditional tools and techniques.

Relief transfer work is uncomplicated and inexpensive. The basic materials are spray paints and ordinary kitchen aluminum foil. Printing is done without a press of any kind.

The method itself is quite simple and easily mastered. Even the first few attempts can produce astonishingly successful results. It is my hope that the reader, having gained pleasure and insight at the start, will be inspired to experiment further and discover the many artistically rewarding experiences that lie ahead.

chapter 1
discovering the three-dimensional surface

When we observe the three-dimensional solidity of the world around us, we experience a special kind of pleasure. We not only enjoy the purely optical delights of color, shape, and contour, but the physical awareness of weight and depth. The sense of touch is present and we are able to feel with our eyes as well as see.

This immediately makes us think of texture, which, like all three-dimensional form, is revealed by light and shadow. When light strikes across a surface, it brings every irregularity into sharp relief, creating a pattern of shadows that is unique to that particular surface. As we can see in the accompanying photograph of a crumpled piece of paper (Fig. 1), the shadows define the texture and tell us that the paper is not flat. If we were to flatten it, the shadows would disappear, and so would the distinctive texture they produce.

If we were able to flatten the paper, and still keep the shadows, the actual three-dimensional form would be lost. However, an illusion of the form would remain on the two-dimensional surface. A simple way to accomplish this is shown in the next photograph (Fig. 2). The crumpled paper is being sprayed with black paint in such a manner that some portions are exposed to the paint while others are not. This is done by spraying horizontally *along* the surface, not directly at it. Note that the light is com-

1 Thin tissue paper was used for this photograph.

2 Spraying along the surface of the paper.

ing from the left; the spraying is therefore done from the right, and the paint strikes only those portions that are in shadow.

When the paper is flattened, the real shadows are gone. They have been replaced by duplicates in paint. If we compare the result (Fig. 3) with the photograph of the actual crumpled paper, we see that a convincing illusion has been created.

Extraordinary results can be obtained with plain white paper and quick-drying black enamel spray paint alone. When a variety of color is used, however, the effect can be quite dramatic. Light colors should be sprayed from the same side to simulate the direction of actual light and dark colors should be sprayed from the opposite side to simulate the positions of actual shadows.

The best way to flatten a finished paper is to cover the back with a water-free adhesive, such as rubber cement, place it on mounting board or construction paper, and press it with a rolling pin.

3 The flattened paper. The exaggerated light and dark contrast is deliberate.

4-6   These are some of the effects that can be obtained
with paper. Tissue paper gives the best results.

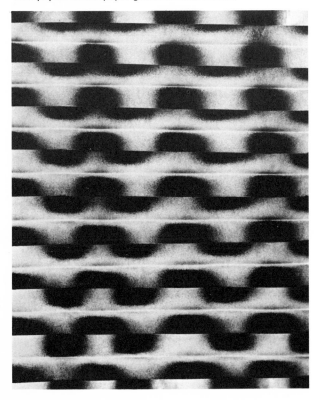

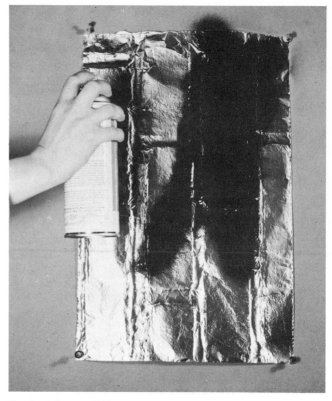

7 Making the foil impression.

8 Applying a solid base coat.

The Aluminum Foil Transfer Process

Gratifying as ordinary paper can be, it is limited to the relatively few and rather similar effects that can be obtained by crumpling, twisting, or folding. In order to go beyond this limitation, we must use a more versatile material. Aluminum foil fills this requirement perfectly. It not only does everything that paper can do, but a great deal more: it can transfer an actual texture to a flat surface, literally translating a relief into a two-dimensional representation of that relief. The resulting *trompe l'oeil* quality is so powerful, at times, that the spectator is tempted to touch the design to see if it is really flat.

Conventional kitchen foil, rather than the heavy duty or quilted kind, should be used. The following three photographs show how this is done. A sheet of foil is pressed over the surface to be transferred, in this case a brick wall. It is rubbed firmly with a piece of soft cloth or a wad of cotton until a clear,

three-dimensional impression of the wall is obtained (Fig. 7). The foil is then carefully pinned to a board and is ready for spraying.

First a solid coat of black, or some other very dark paint, is sprayed directly over the entire surface (Fig. 8). This guarantees covering all of the deeply recessed spots likely to be missed by the colors that come later. And, since these recessed places are normally in shadow anyway, the dark paint will make them appear correctly as shadows in the finished design.

When this base coat is dry, and no unpainted foil is visible, the various other dark and light colors can be sprayed on. As with the crumpled paper, the paint should be sprayed at a sharply raking angle along the surface of the foil (Fig. 9). The dark and light colors should, of course, be sprayed from opposite directions.

When the paint is thoroughly dry, the foil is placed

9 Spraying the light and dark colors.

10 Flattening the painted foil.

on a table. It is first pressed and patted flat by hand, then rolled flat with a rolling pin (Fig. 10). While pressing by hand, it is important not to smooth the wrinkles by stretching the foil, but to press straight down with a crushing motion that will not change the relative positions of lights and shadows. Smoothing and stretching would simply unpleat the design, causing surface distortion and spoiling the illusion.

After being completely flattened with the rolling pin, the finished design is an exact duplicate of the brick surface (Fig. 11). Notice how faithfully every detail has been preserved, and how similar the result is to a photograph.

Almost any kind of surface can be duplicated in this fashion. There is only one major limitation: the surface must be in low relief. Aluminum foil is not sufficiently elastic to stretch evenly over high bumps, or into the deep valleys between them. If forced, the foil will tend to wrinkle and tear. It pays to experi-

11 Finished transfer design.

ment, and, through trial and error, discover which types of surface are the best.

It doesn't matter how shallow the relief is. Even the faintest details can be brought out with careful angling of the spray paint, and with the use of strongly contrasting light and dark colors. The depth of relief in the wood grain shown here (Fig. 12) is no more than one thirty-second of an inch. It appears to be much deeper because of the deliberate exaggeration of light and shadow.

Once the basic transfer technique is mastered, experimentation follows naturally. One can literally invent effects of color and light that are rarely found in nature, and still retain a photographic illusion of reality. The same textured surface can even be used over and over again, each time with entirely different results. Different uses of light and color can effect many transformations of the same surface.

A rather interesting optical illusion occasionally crops up in transfer work. A finished design will sometimes seem to undergo a sudden inversion of form accompanied by a complete reversal in the direction of light. Holes will turn into bumps, and bumps into holes. Photographs of the moon's surface often produce this kind of illusion—craters unexpectedly becoming inflated domes, and ridges collapsing into deep ravines. Then, without warning, everything snaps back to normal. The illusion can be noted in the following photograph (Fig. 13). The two ''moon'' closeups are transfer designs made from the same plaster bas-relief. They are identical, except that in one the light is coming from the left, and in the other the light is coming from the right. The eye cannot adjust to both directions at the same time, so it accepts only one, and applies it to both images. The result is that one of the moons has craters, while the other has domes. If the eye suddenly switches to the other light direction, which can happen momentarily, the craters and domes change place accordingly.

The illusion can be controlled to some extent. If a particular design persists in flopping into reverse too readily, stand next to a lamp or window in such a way that the direction of actual light coincides with the simulated light in the design. In many cases this will compel the eye to ''read'' the image the way it was intended.

On the following pages are examples of other textures that have been transferred to aluminum foil. Any optical illusions that may occur are purely accidental.

12 On the left: photograph of a piece of wood. On the right: flattened transfer design made from it.

13 To make this illusion work, stand next to a lamp or window with the light coming either from the left or the right. Stare fixedly at one of the moons for about ten seconds, then do the same with the other moon. Shift your gaze back and forth in this manner; in less than a minute the holes in one of the moons should suddenly turn into bumps. If you quickly turn the picture upside down at this point, the effect will be reversed.

14, 15 An example of bark, left, and the transfer made from it.

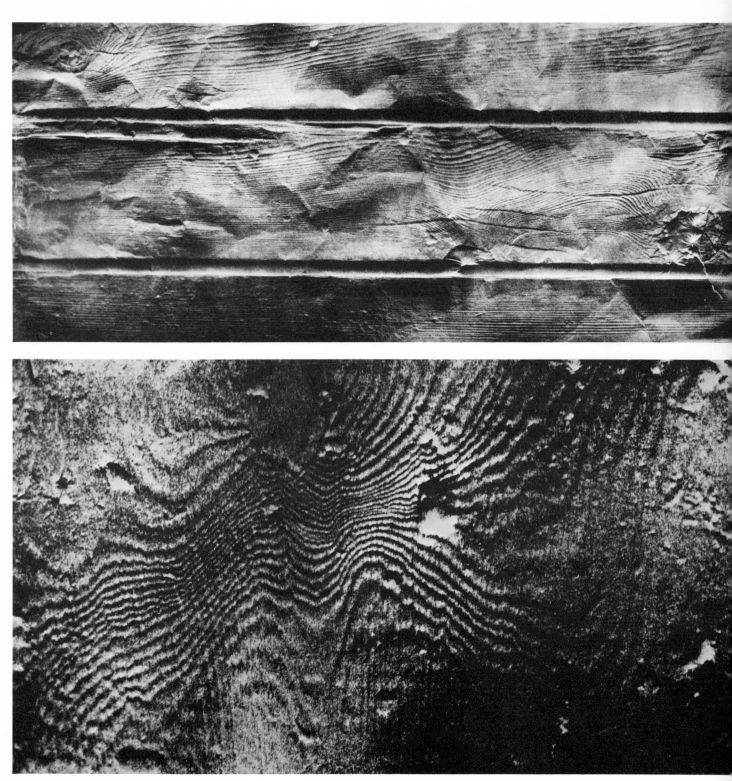

16, 17 Wood-grain transfers.

18 This design was made from a manhole cover.

19 Congealed tar on a rooftop provided the surface for this relief transfer.

Mounting

Finished aluminum transfer designs should not be glued flat to mounting board or paper, as is done with crumpled paper designs. If this is done, the foil will wrinkle and buckle within a few hours, because of room temperature changes causing the metal to expand and contract. Only the edges of the design should be taped or glued to the board, and one small spot should be kept open so that air will not be trapped between the foil and the board.

If a matt frame is desired, it is best to glue the design directly to the back of the "window". A piece of cardboard can then be used for backing. It should not be glued to the foil, but only to the matt frame.

Unfortunately, even when it is carefully mounted and matted, the aluminum foil design is not as permanent as it should be. The slightest mishandling can cause the foil to tear, or the paint to flake off. Repairs are discouragingly difficult to make.

Obviously the only way to solve this problem is to get rid of the foil and somehow keep the design. How this can be done is described in the next chapter.

20 Block of strongly grained wood, together with its
aluminum foil impression.

chapter 2
transfer prints
and multiples

Transfer printing is a most rewarding experience. Finished prints are remarkably clear, full-bodied, and richly-toned. Every detail of texture and color is captured with absolute fidelity. Unlike lithography, etching, block printing, or serigraphy, each print has the highly individual character of a finely executed painting. Color, light, and shadow are blended with the smoothness and subtlety of perfectly controlled brush work.

Indeed, each print *is* a painting in its own right. It is not a stamped image taken from an inked surface, but the actual painted design removed from the aluminum foil and transferred to paper or some other material. No press is necessary.

There are several methods of printing which proceed from the same basic technique: the flattened foil design is pressed, paint side down, to a strongly adhesive surface. The foil is then peeled away, leaving the paint stuck to the adhesive surface which has more gripping power than the slick surface of the foil. The various methods are as follows:

Face-down Print

Like etching or block printing, this produces a reverse image. First, a relief surface is chosen, such as the one shown here (Fig. 20). Next, the aluminum foil impression is made. It is then sprayed, but not in the usual manner; this time, the all-covering first coat (described in Chapter 1) is put on last. We start with our light and dark colors, carefully applying a little of each: some dark colors, then some light colors; more dark and more light; and so on until the foil is completely covered. Remember to spray along the surface of the foil to keep the lights and darks from invading one another's territory. Bear in mind that, when the print is made, only those colors that are in direct contact with the foil will be seen; any paint that goes over these colors will be hidden under them in the final print. In other words, it is the initial spraying that counts.

When the paint is dry, the foil is flattened with a rolling pin in the customary manner (Fig. 10, Chapter 1). It can then be sprayed with a final solid coat of the same color as the darkest one used in the initial spraying. Though not absolutely necessary, this serves to thicken the entire paint surface, particularly those places that may have been missed. The final coat will not be noticeable in the print, since it will end up underneath the colors that were put on first.

21 Spraying the construction paper.

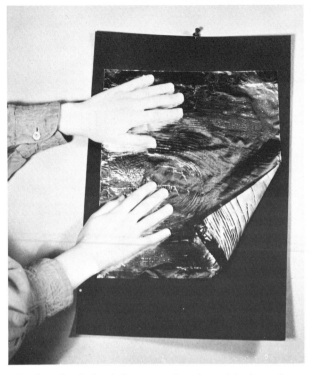

22 Transfer design being pressed against sticky face of construction paper.

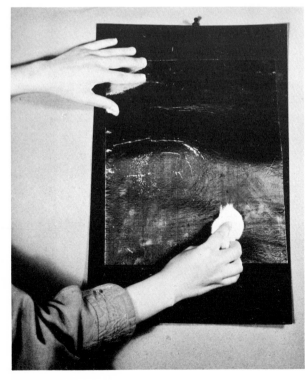

23 Rubbing the foil.

24 Burnishing the foil. Note the corners separating from the paint.

Now the print can be made. Select a sheet of construction paper slightly larger than the foil design to allow trimming later on. Black is best because it conceals any small imperfections that may appear. Apply adhesive, coating the surface evenly with a thin film (Fig. 21). While it is drying, test it occasionally with your finger. When it is no longer wet, but simply very tacky like masking tape for example, it is ready for printing.

Place the construction paper on a table, sticky side up; flatten the foil design with a rolling pin and smooth it so that it is perfectly flat. Next, press it paint side down over the construction paper, smoothing and flattening it by hand. When this is done, the paper and the foil will be stuck together (Fig. 22). The final solid coat of paint has been purposely omitted in the example shown here so that the design can be seen on the partly exposed underside of the foil.

With a wad of cotton, rub the foil until it is glued down as flat and smooth as possible (Fig. 23). Then cut away the excess construction paper. Repeat the rubbing process, bearing down hard. A little talcum powder sprinkled over the foil beforehand will make this easier. Pockets of trapped air resembling small blisters sometimes appear at this point; these can be punctured with a fine needle and flattened without affecting the print in any way.

Next, using the flat of a paint scraper, stroke the surface of the foil, squeegee fashion, working out from the center and over the edge. When the entire surface has been burnished in this manner, repeat the process until the foil begins to separate from the construction paper. This usually occurs first at one of the corners (Fig. 24). With the aid of tweezers, the foil can now be peeled off. If everything has been done correctly, the foil will come away perfectly clean, leaving the design intact on the paper (Fig. 25).

25   The last bit of foil is removed from the print.

Face-up Print

This method provides an image that is not reversed. The print is identical to the painted foil design in every detail. Start by making the foil impression, then spray on a base coat of paint as described in Chapter 1. When this is dry, the light and dark colors can be applied. When the entire design is completely dry, it is flattened with a rolling pin. Now place it paint side up on a slightly larger piece of paper, smooth it out, and tape down the corners, covering as little of each corner as possible (Fig. 26). Set it aside.

Next, take a piece of transparent, self-adhesive plastic, slightly larger than the paper on which the design is taped. Con-Tact brand transparent plastic is the best. Remove the protective backing and tack the plastic, adhesive side up, to a piece of wood or cardboard. This is the hardest part of the entire operation. Con-Tact is quite sticky; once you are holding it, it is difficult to let go. Unless you are extremely careful, you may find yourself acting out one of those old silent film comedy routines in which the unfortunate hero gets tangled up in flypaper. The best way to do it is to peel away the backing along one edge to expose an inch or two of the clear plastic. Tack this end down, then peel away the rest of the backing, almost to the end, and tack that end down. The remainder of the backing can then be removed (Fig. 27).

Now place the design paint side down, flat against the adhesive surface of the Con-Tact (Fig. 28). Smooth it down firmly and trim away the excess Con-Tact. When the design is turned over, it can be seen through the clear plastic. You can now trim everything that is not part of the design. Remove the paper on which it is taped.

26 Foil design being taped down at corners. A tile wall provided the original relief surface.

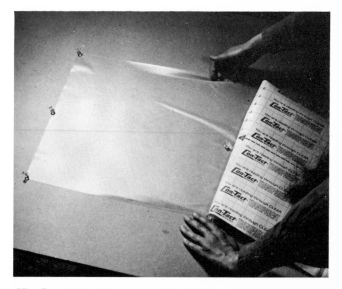

27 Completing the removal of the backing. The end of the Con-Tact has already been tacked down.

24

28 Placing the foil design against sticky surface of Con-Tact.

At this stage the design will appear somewhat cloudy and indistinct because it is not yet adhering closely enough to the Con-Tact. Energetic rubbing with a piece of clean cotton will bring the design to its fullest clarity (Fig. 29). When this has been done, it can be turned over and stroked with the flat of a paint scraper as in the previously discussed face-down print (Fig. 30); and, as before, the foil will begin to separate from the Con-Tact and can be peeled off. The print should then be glued to a piece of black construction paper, after which it can be matted or mounted in whatever manner is desired.

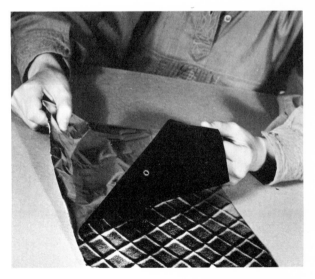

30 Removing the foil. The black underside of the print is the base coat.

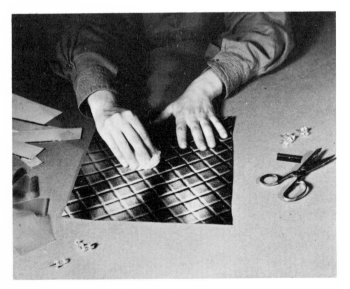

29 Rubbing with a wad of cotton.

32 Applying polymer to sheet of acetate.

31 Covering foil design with polymer gloss medium. Initial foil impression was made from some dry, cracked tar on a rooftop.

26

Face-up Print on Acetate

This method produces the best print of all. Start with the foil impression as usual. Spray it with a base coat, apply your light and dark colors, let the paint dry, and flatten the design with a rolling pin.

Place the design face up on a larger piece of paper, smooth it out, and tape down the corners. Now, using a wide, flat brush with soft, closely packed bristles, cover the design with a thin coat of undiluted polymer liquid gloss medium (Fig. 31). The gloss is important because it remains slightly tacky when dry. The brush strokes should be parallel and should extend unbroken across the surface of the design. As soon as this is finished, and before the polymer has had a chance to dry, carefully re-move the design from the paper to which it is taped, and set it aside. A sheet of ten point acetate, larger than the design, is then prepared with a coat of polymer in exactly the same way (Fig. 32).

When the design and the acetate are both dry, they are pressed face to face (Fig. 33). Working on the foil side, use a wad of cotton to smooth out the design and bring it into maximum contact with the polymer surface of the acetate. The foil is then bur-nished with the flat of a paint scraper, as before, until it begins to separate from the acetate. It can then be peeled free, leaving the design printed on the acetate (Fig. 34).

This type of printing can also be done on Plexiglas.

33 Placing foil and acetate face to face.

34 After being rubbed with cotton, and burnished with a paint scraper, the foil is peeled away.

35 Pressing the design face down on to the second piece of foil.

36 The double sheet has been trimmed and burnished. The first piece of foil is being peeled away, leaving its design, face down, on the second piece.

Offset Print

This involves a rather demanding *modus operandi* consisting of two steps: transferring the original foil design to another piece of foil; and transferring the design from that piece of foil to a piece of material. Interestingly, nothing is lost in this double translation.

After being sprayed and flattened in the already familiar manner, the foil design is placed, paint side up, on a larger sheet of paper, and taped down at the corners. It is then given a thin coat of polymer gloss medium exactly as described in the preceding method. Before the polymer is dry, remove the design from the paper it is on and set it aside. Take a clean, smooth, unused piece of foil and coat it with polymer the same way.

When both the design and the second piece of foil are dry, press them together face to face. Vigorous rubbing with a piece of cotton will cause the two tacky polymer surfaces to fuse (Fig. 35). Next, place this double sheet flat on a board with the second piece of foil on the bottom. Stroke the top sheet with the flat of a paint scraper until the foil begins to separate from its design. It can then be peeled away. The design will remain, face down, on the bottom piece of foil. All you will see will be the base coat; the design will be concealed under it, facing the foil (Fig. 36).

This piece of foil is now placed on a large piece of paper, paint side up, and taped down at the corners. It is then given a thick coat of polymer liquid gloss medium (Fig. 37). While the polymer is still quite wet, cover it with a piece of cotton or linen material. Bed sheeting is excellent. Then, with a wide brush, cover the material with polymer, brushing it in until there are no dry spots. While doing this, gently "iron" out all wrinkles (Fig. 38).

When this preliminary soaking and smoothing is finished, and while the polymer is still wet, take a piece of cardboard with a straight edge and squeegee across the surface of the material. Try to get the material perfectly flat—no wrinkles or air bubbles. It should be in full contact with the foil and the polymer should be spread evenly. Allow it to dry, undisturbed, for twenty-four hours. When it is thoroughly dry, trim it; the foil can then be peeled away and the design will remain, face up, on the material.

The peeling is, unpredictably, sometimes easy and sometimes difficult. The hardest part is getting started; after that it usually goes slowly, though

28

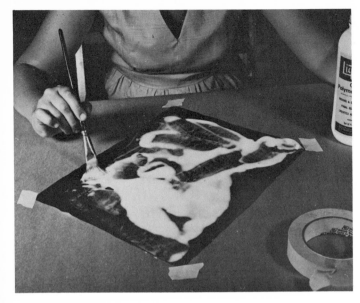

37 Applying polymer to second piece of foil.

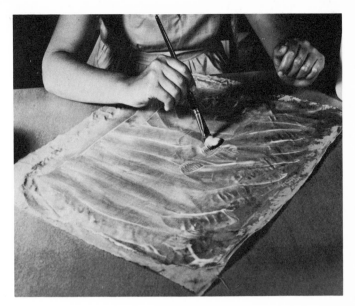

38 Brushing the polymer into the material.

surely, toward a successful conclusion. It is necessary to work carefully, using fine tweezers to get between the foil and the paint, and to pull away the foil (Fig. 39).

These prints can be made on a variety of materials: illustration board; strong, heavy paper such as Bristol board, wood, primed and unprimed canvas. The only requirements are that the surface be fairly smooth and porous enough to permit the polymer to dry thoroughly.

When printing is done on inflexible surfaces such as wood, the polymer should be applied both to the foil design and the surface of the wood. The two wet surfaces are then brought together and the squeegeeing is done on the foil. Care should be taken to get the foil perfectly smooth and flat without tearing or scoring it. No air bubbles or excess polymer should remain between the foil and the wood.

Face-down prints can also be made with polymer. The foil is first prepared in the manner described at the beginning of this chapter. It is then printed directly on the desired material exactly as in offset printing. There is, of course, no need to transfer it to another sheet of foil first.

39 Stripping away the foil.

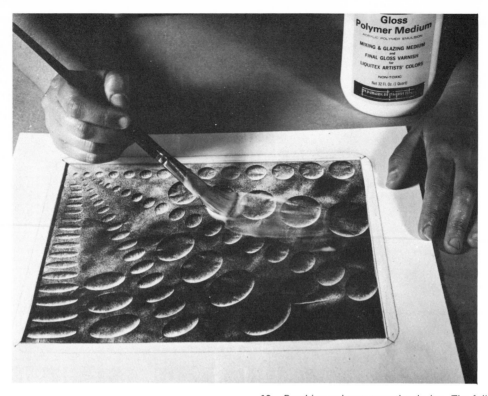

40 Brushing polymer over the design. The foil impression came from an ellipse template, a device commonly used in drafting.

Decalcomania Method

This is an excellent way to make small prints up to approximately 12″ x 14″. Start with the painted, flattened foil design. Smooth it so that it is perfectly flat with no wrinkling or buckling. Cut a matt window, cover the back with adhesive, and place it over the design as if you were framing it permanently. Press it down so that it makes perfect contact with the foil. Now, brush on a thick coat of polymer gloss medium with long, parallel strokes. Work up to, and even slightly over, the edges and corners of the matt frame (Fig. 40). When this coat is thoroughly dry, apply a second coat the same way. Repeat the process until you have built up a tough skin four or five layers thick.

If you wish, you can use polymer gel instead of polymer gloss medium, since it works just as well. Apply a thick coat of gel as smoothly as possible and allow it to dry overnight. Apply a second coat of gel and allow that to dry overnight also. When completely dry, the gel will be a skin covering the foil design.

Dry polymer, whether gel or gloss medium, is perfectly transparent. A clear and lustrous design is seen through it. First cut the design out of the matt frame; then, working carefully with fine tweezers, remove the foil. Peel the foil off slowly without tearing the skin. Don't worry if the skin stretches out of shape; it will return to normal in a few minutes after the peeling is completed. The print can then be glued to a piece of construction paper, or other strong backing, and matted as desired.

A few words of caution: when peeling away the foil, and, subsequently, when mounting the print, be careful not to let the polymer skin flop over, fold, or in any other way cause its face to come in contact with itself. As we have seen, polymer remains quite tacky even after it has dried. When dry polymer surfaces meet, they stick together and it is sometimes impossible to separate them. Once the print is mounted, the danger is more or less eliminated. Be sure, however, never to stack or pile polymer prints or paintings face to face.

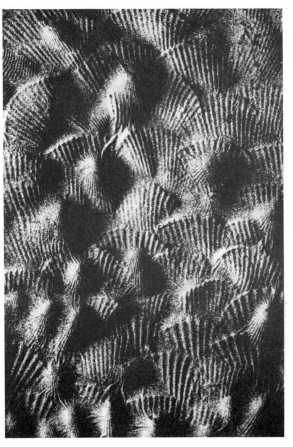

41 Single value prints. The relief surface was a plaster cast made from a sheet of clay into which scallop shells had been pressed. Plaster surfaces, and how to prepare them, are discussed in the next chapter.

Single Value Printing

No base coat and no final coat are used with this method. After the foil impression is made, one or more colors are sprayed along the foil from one direction only. If they are dark colors, they will function as shadows; if they are light colors, they will function as light. Foil that is unpainted is left blank. For best results in printing, use the face-up Con-Tact method described earlier in this chapter.

Finished prints must be mounted on construction paper that contrasts strongly in value with the color used in the print. Figure 41 shows two such prints. The one on the left was made with a single dark color and mounted on white paper; the one on the right was made with a single light color and mounted on black paper. Note that even when one color is used, strong chiaroscuro can still be achieved.

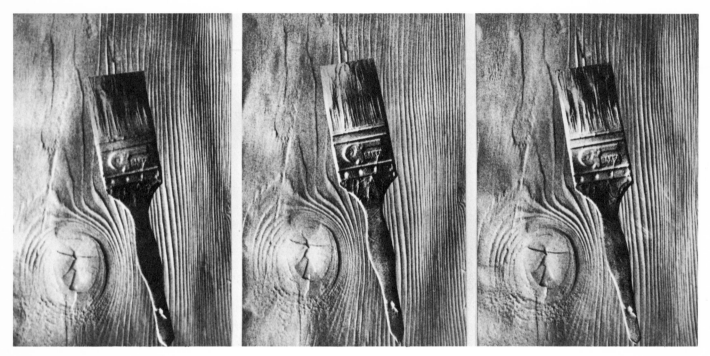

42 Three face-up prints done on transparent Con-Tact.

Multiples

Since the transfer process requires a relief surface of some kind to begin with, obviously more than one transfer can be made. The surface serves as a template from which an unlimited number of copies can be produced. They will all be identical in form, but will vary from one another in the way that the paint is applied. With proper control, these variations can be minimized.

Suppose you are putting out an edition of forty multiples. If you want them to be as much alike as possible, you must systematize your work by breaking it down into a few simple operations that can easily be duplicated in every print. You should start with a good prototype, the print that will serve as a model for all the rest. From that point on, work on as many designs as possible at the same time. Spray on all of the base coats first, all of the blues next, then all of the yellows, and so on. In each design the prototype should be followed exactly: same angle of spray; same amount of each color; same location for each color. With care, one can produce a great many prints that are almost exactly alike. The three prints shown here will give some idea of the degree of success that can be achieved this way (Fig. 42).

Some Final Suggestions

Every finished design should have a wide enough border to allow for proper matting or for any trimming that may be necessary. This can be accomplished at the very start, when making the initial foil impression, by using a piece of foil that is larger than the intended design. Then, when spraying, make certain that the paint covers this border area.

The paper, cardboard, or material on which the print is being made should always be larger than the piece of foil. It can subsequently be trimmed down to the size of the foil. This makes the burnishing and peeling of the foil relatively easy. Sheets of hard plastic or wood are difficult to trim. If you wish to print on such surfaces, you must plan accordingly.

The purpose of burnishing is twofold: to make the foil design as flat as possible, thus bringing the paint into total contact with the adhesive surface; and to loosen the paint from the foil so that the foil can be removed as cleanly as possible. A paint scraper is excellent for this purpose but other tools are just as good: a piece of wood or stiff cardboard with a smooth straight edge; a piece of stiff plastic; the back of a spoon. A single-edged razor blade can also be used but, for obvious reasons, it is not recommended for children. If it must be used, it should be inserted into a special holder, many varieties of which are available in art supply and hardware stores. This precaution applies not only to burnishing, but to trimming of designs and other kinds of cutting as well.

This chapter has dealt with the three basic methods of relief transfer printing: the face-down print, the face-up print viewed through a transparent surface; and the face-up offset print. Several interesting variations of these methods, along with a sampling of related designs, will be considered in the next chapter.

43 This texture was made with salt.

chapter 3
design

The unique optical effects associated with relief transfer work are, happily, built-in characteristics of the process itself. Striking illusion and color appear effortlessly, almost magically, at the very start. Once such a technique is mastered, it can become a versatile tool for shaping meaningful and complex pictorial ideas.

In many cases, such ideas begin with the particular relief surface from which the transfer design is made. For this reason, it is useful to know how to create original surfaces and not depend on those provided by nature alone. Such surfaces can be made in different ways, from inventing textures to the making of complete *bas-relief* sculptures. Here are a few suggestions:

Homemade Textures
Unusual surfaces can be fabricated by spreading glue on a piece of wood or cardboard and sprinkling it with sand or salt. Variations can be introduced by adding different kinds of grain, cereal, or fine gravel. There is much room for experimentation with such materials. (Fig. 43.)

Using Found Objects
Objects that are not too thick, such as coins, keys, string, and washers, can be glued to a board and used as a template. If the pieces are arranged expressively and if color and light are used with imagination, the result can be quite satisfactory. Other objects that can be used are: applicator sticks; pieces of spaghetti (uncooked, of course); paper clips; hairpins—anything, in fact, that can produce a design in low relief.

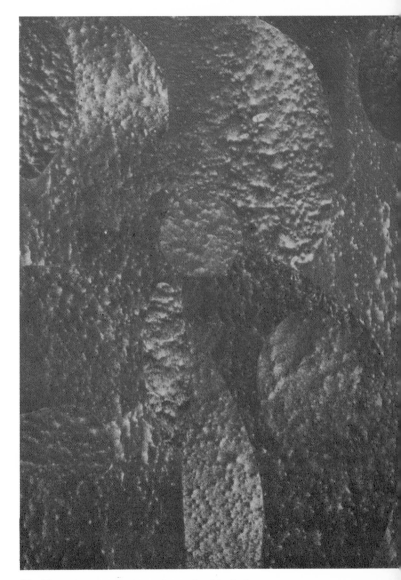

44 The salt texture was used to make this design.

Cutouts

Thin balsa wood, about one-sixteenth of an inch thick, can easily be cut into any desired shape and glued to a board (Fig. 45). The resulting transfer designs are sharp and clear. The terrace pattern shown here is an example (Fig. 46).

46 Print made from a balsa wood relief.

45 A design being cut out of thin balsa wood. At the left is a relief made of found objects glued to cardboard.

48 The surface used for this print was made by gluing thin sticks of balsa wood to a piece of cardboard.

47 This design was made from a construction paper relief.

49 String was the object used to make this print.

50 Modeling a surface with polymer gel and plastic knife.

51 Print made from a modeled surface.

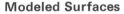

52 Making a three-dimensional drawing with glue.

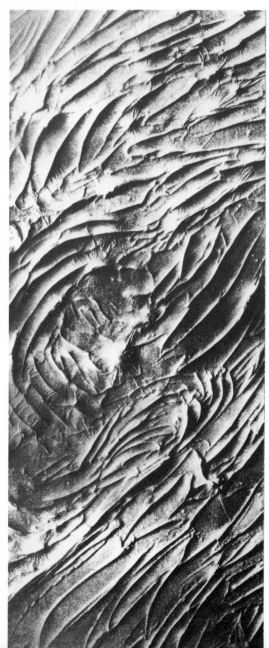

Modeled Surfaces

These are the best surfaces to work from. Not only can the finished relief be an original concept, but its thickness can be controlled to produce the best possible foil impression. Beautifully free abstract forms can be obtained by spreading polymer modeling paste on a board and working into it with a palette knife or some other tool. Polymer gel and polymer gesso can be used in similar fashion (Fig. 50). Delightful three-dimensional drawings can be made by squeezing glue onto a board. Polymer gesso, applied with a squeeze-bottle, will produce the same results (Fig. 52).

The best way to model a surface is to make it out of clay, either plasticine or moist clay, then cast it in plaster of paris. The plaster is used as the template. The "moon" print discussed in Chapter 1 was done this way. (See Fig. 13.)

Clay surfaces can be shaped in two different ways. The design can be done in reverse, incised with tools or by hand. Plaster is then poured over it and allowed to set. When the hardened plaster is removed, it will be a "positive" impression of the "negative" clay design. The foil impression is then made from the plaster (Figs. 53, 54, 55).

The other method involves modeling the clay as a "positive" design to begin with—in other words, simply as a relief. When plaster is poured over this, the result is a "negative" design. Foil can then be pressed into this mold to make an impression which, when seen from the other side, is actually a "positive". It is this positive side that is sprayed. (Fig. 56.)

53 Making an incised clay "negative".

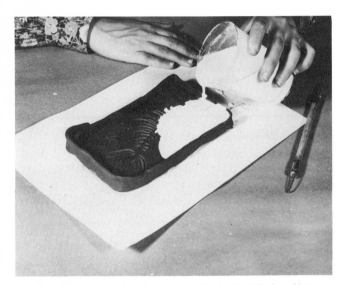

54 Pouring plaster of paris over the incised design. Note the clay retaining wall around the design; this prevents the plaster from overflowing.

55 At the right: the plaster has set and has been removed from the clay. It is now a "positive" relief. The print made from it is at the left.

56 This negative plaster mold was made by pouring plaster of paris over an actual fish. Figure 71 is a design made from foil impressions of this and another similar mold.

One important suggestion applies to all of the homemade textures and reliefs described here: before making the foil impression, dust the relief surface with talcum powder. This will eliminate all vestiges of tackiness from whatever glue, polymer, or plaster may have been used. There will then be no danger of the foil impression sticking to its surface once it has been rubbed and is ready to be removed. The dusting is best accomplished with the aid of a large, soft-bristled brush.

57 Several household objects provided the relief surface for this stretched foil print.

Stretched Foil

In instances where an illusion of higher relief is needed, the foil should be prepared in the following manner before the impression is made: crumple the sheet of foil thoroughly until it is wrinkled and contracted into an evenly distributed granular texture. Press it flat, without unpleating it, and roll it as smoothly as possible with a rolling pin. Because of the myriad of tiny folds in its surface, the foil now possesses enough slack, or flexibility, to enable it to stretch more comfortably over bumps and into depressions. When such foil is sprayed, the paint takes on a slightly coarse, matt-like appearance, something like sandpaper or unpolished stone (Fig. 57). An outstanding feature of this type of foil is the ease with which it can be freely shaped by hand.

The best printing results with this stretchable foil can be made with the face-up method on either Con-Tact or acetate. Don't be discouraged by the appearance of the print when the foil is stripped away. It will look like a total disaster. The rough surface of the foil will not have made full contact with the adhesive, and, consequently, there will be a great many blank spots. All you have to do is mount the print on a piece of paper that is the same color, or as close to it as possible, as the darkest shadow color in the print. All of the imperfections will disappear magically and the design will come alive. And, if you examine the finished print closely, you will be amazed at the variety and detail of texture you have created (Fig. 58).

It is advisable not to print stretched foil designs with any of the wet polymer methods, such as decalcomania or offset. The extremely rough surface of

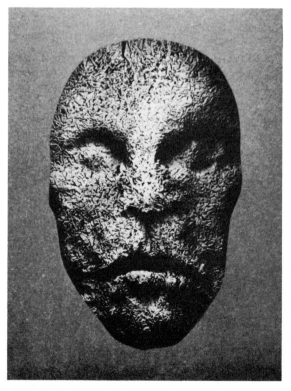

58 A mask, modeled by hand in stretched foil, often produces such a strong photographic illusion, it is hard to believe that it is a perfectly flat print.

the foil makes it difficult to remove from the printing surface without damaging the design. If a wet polymer method must be used for some special reason, however, the foil should be made as smooth and flat as possible before printing.

Montage Designs

No material or technique is perfect. The artist accepts this as a fact of life and learns to compensate for the limitations of his medium and, at the same time, exploit its virtues to the fullest.

Relief transfer is no exception to this general rule; along with its good qualities it possesses a few shortcomings which can, on occasion, be somewhat frustrating. Fortunately, they can be handled easily.

One of these shortcomings is the difficulty of clearly showing where one color ends and another begins. Spray paint cannot be controlled with the accuracy of a brush; some of the color intended for one particular part of a design invariably drifts over into a neighboring area where it is not wanted.

There are several ways to get around this problem, one of which is shown here (Fig. 59). This design, after having been printed on transparent Con-Tact (see Chapter 2), was found to be unsatisfactory because of insufficient contrast between the main figure and its background. The figure was therefore cut out in one piece and mounted on a sheet of illustration board that had first been painted to best provide the desired contrast. Compare the result with Figure 60. In this example, the absence of distinct color separation is purposely intended to suggest that figure and background together are a single object, relatively uniform in value and color.

59 A number of different surfaces were used to create the various textures seen here.

60 A companion piece to Figure 55.

61 Collage design made from fragments of Con-Tact prints.

With this cutout montage method, designs of great complexity and detail can be devised. Figure 61, for example, was made with dozens of cutouts snipped from many different prints. The cutouts were glued to a dark blue contrasting background. Figure 62 is another example of this type of montage. The human figures in this design were made from loosely shaped foil. No templates were used. The foil was sculptured directly by hand, sprayed, flattened, and printed on Con-Tact in the usual manner.

The cutout method produces a definite collage effect that is quite interesting. The glued-on shapes provide an overall actual texture that works well with the illusory texture present in each piece. The result is an attractive, eye-catching surface quality.

When a perfectly smooth surface is preferred, however, all of the shapes should be cut out of the painted foil transfer *before* they are printed. Figure 64 is an example of a foil montage that was first glued together to form the complete design, then printed in one piece. A sheet of sprayed foil was used as a background. Several cutout foil shapes were then individually covered on the back with adhesive and glued flat against the background. The finished design was made as smooth and flat as possible and then printed.

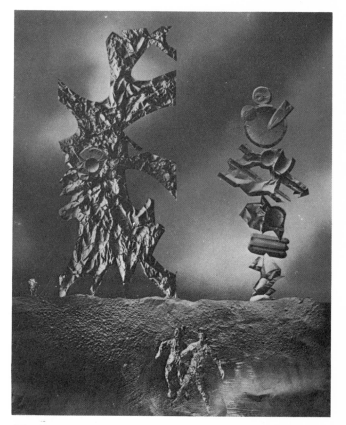

62 Another Con-Tact collage.

63, 64 Prints made from foil montages.

It should be pointed out here that the printing techniques used for montages are no different from those already described in Chapter 2. No matter how complicated a montage may be, it is, for all practical purposes, a single sheet of foil. It can thus be printed in any of the ways already familiar to the reader. Special care should be taken, nevertheless, in this respect: cutouts should be glued down perfectly flat, particularly when polymer medium is to be used; if cutouts are glued down loosely, polymer can seep under them and cause possible damage to the final print while the foil is being removed. Also, avoid gluing too many cutouts on top of one another. This can create mounds of foil, here and there, whose extra thickness prevents the immediately surrounding paint from making proper contact with the adhesive. This problem does not arise with the decalcomania method; since the adhesive surface in this case is brush-applied polymer, there is little danger of its missing any part of the design.

65 For best results, the spray can should be held approximately eight inches away from the paper.

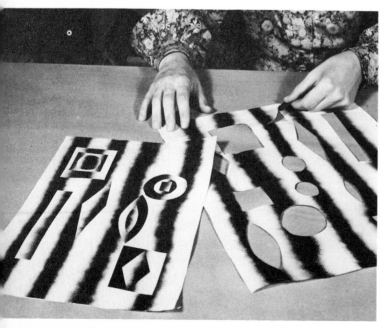

66 Making a non-relief design.

Non-relief Design

This final variation, strictly speaking, doesn't belong in this book because no relief surfaces are involved. It does require the use of foil and spray paint, however, and the foil design can be printed in any of the ways already described.

Start by pinning two perfectly smooth pieces of foil to a board and spraying each one with a solid base coat of some light color. Next, using dark colors, spray lines on both pieces of foil as shown in Figure 65. One of these pieces is the work sheet, the other will be the design.

Cut a shape out of the worksheet in such a way that it is dark along one side and light along the opposite side. The back of this cutout is then glued to the design so that its dark edge is set against a light background color, and its light edge is set against a dark background. An illusion of three-dimensional form occurs immediately. Glue on more shapes, constantly placing lights and darks against one another. Cutouts can be superimposed over one another to create variety and to heighten the effect of light and shadow (Fig. 66). Keep adding to the design in this way until it is finished. It can then be printed. Figure 67 is an example of a non-relief print.

These designs, incidentally, are equally effective with paper. Light colored paper should be used. White paper and black spray paint alone will produce fine results (Fig. 68).

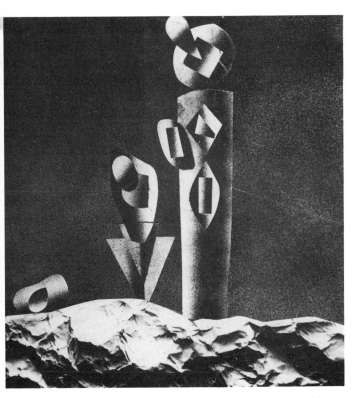

67 The non-relief technique was used to create the objects in this landscape. The foreground was made from crumpled foil.

68 An example of a non-relief design made with paper.

Glazing with Oils and Acrylics

There are many brands of quick-drying spray paint on the market and most of these are quite good for relief transfer purposes. Unfortunately, the selection of colors is limited to standard primaries and secondaries and very little else. Mixing of these colors must be done directly on the design, but this method rarely produces the desired result. Working with canned spray paint alone, the artist is restricted to a painfully inadequate palette.

Hand-mixed lacquers and enamels, applied with an air brush or some other paint-spraying device, could provide all of the colors that are not available in spray cans. This would require, besides an outlay of money, considerable time in the preparation of paint and the cleaning of equipment.

The simplest and, possibly, the most effective way to expand the spray paint palette is to paint with a brush directly over the transfer design with whatever colors are desired. Either oils or acrylics, both of which come in a full range of colors, can be used. For best results, the paint should be applied to the foil design and allowed to dry thoroughly *before* printing. Except in certain cases which will be mentioned later, paint should not be used on the finished print.

The Glazing Technique

With both acrylics and oils, glazing consists of thinning the color to a transparent consistency and applying it in a wash that permits the spray paint underneath to show through (Fig. 69). This serves to enrich a design by adding subtle tonalities, changing some colors, and intensifying the brilliance of others. A foil design that has been made with nothing but black and white spray paint can be con-

69 Glazing. Note that, despite the darkness of the color being used, the underpainting shows through.

verted into a full-blown color composition without losing its underlying form. This method, incidentally, is derived from the old master technique of starting with a light monochromatic underpainting and then glazing over it with transparent colors. This is not unlike the process of color-tinting a black and white photograph. In a transfer design, the effect is one of luminosity and lustrous color.

Glazing With Oils

For glazing purposes, oil paint should be thinned with turpentine. Linseed oil is not recommended because it dries too slowly and does not adhere well to the printing adhesives. Before the foil design can be glazed, the spray paint must be absolutely dry. Otherwise, it will smear and be dissolved by

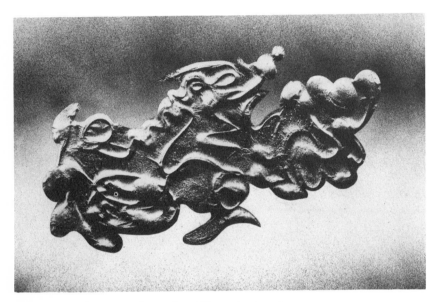

70 Cutout print mounted on painted illustration board.

71 Cutout print.

the turpentine. The oil paint, in turn, must be completely dry before the print can be made. It is advisable to use a soft-haired brush, preferably sable, for glazing.

When turpentine is applied to a smooth, non-absorbent surface like glass, Plexiglas, acetate, or Con-Tact, it takes a long time to dry and tends to leave a resinous residue which remains tacky for an indefinite period. For this reason, glazing should not be done on such surfaces after the print has been made. Results may be attractive but such prints collect dust and are difficult to store and handle.

This rule does not apply to face-down and offset prints, since they do not involve any of the non-absorbent materials just mentioned. Their paint surfaces are uncovered and can be glazed safely.

72 Stretched foil mask print mounted on wood-grain background.

73 The coins above were printed with the decalcomania method, then cut out individually and mounted on white paper. The distortion was achieved by stretching some of the printed "skins" out of shape while gluing them to the paper. See Chapter 2.

74 Terrace designs printed on Con-Tact.

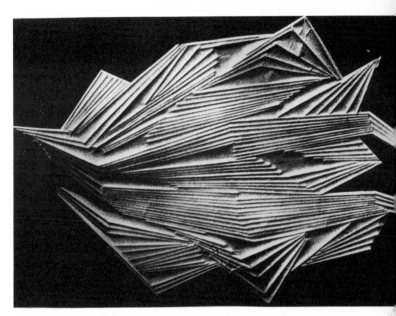

75 Cutout mounted on painted illustration board.
Applicator sticks were used to make the relief for this print.

Glazing With Acrylics

Acrylic paints should be thinned with polymer gloss medium or polymer gel. If water is used, it should be used sparingly and never without polymer. All of the plastic materials used in transfer printing tend to reject water based paints. Polymer medium and gel adhere fairly well to these surfaces. Like oils, acrylic glazes are bright and transparent.

Unlike oils, acrylics can be glazed either over the foil design before printing or over the plastic face of the finished print. Personal preference will determine which method is better.

In both oil and acrylic glazing, all colors work best where the undercolor is light. Dark undercolors become murky when glazed over with light colors such as yellow or orange. Dark glazes have little or no effect on dark undercolors.

49

Opaque Painting

Opaque acrylics can be used either on the foil design before printing or on the plastic face of the final print. If used on the foil, they should be brushed on as flat and smooth as possible.

Opaque oils cannot be used on the foil because they will not print properly. They can, however, be used on the finished print. If this is done, as little turpentine as possible should be mixed with the paint. The design can then be worked on as though it were an ordinary oil painting. Extremely interesting results can be obtained this way.

77 Another cutout print made from an applicator stick relief.

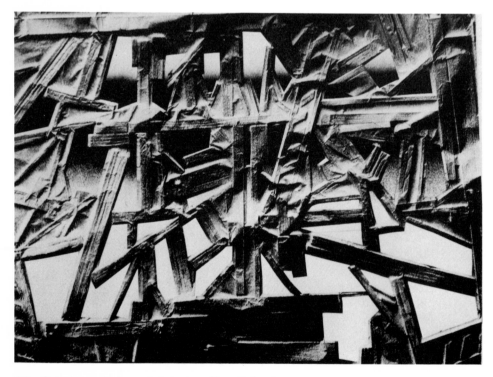

76 Cutout mounted on painted paper. The relief surface was made from balsa wood.

78 Montage print on acetate. The relief was made from
sticks of balsa wood.

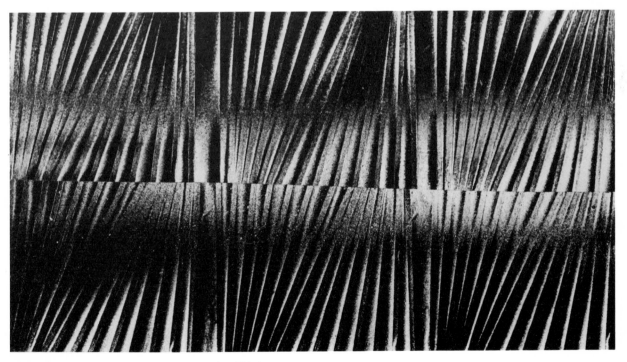

79 Another balsa wood relief montage print. This is a
face-down print on construction paper. See Chapter 2.

Transparencies

The usual way to spray a foil impression, as we know, is to spray dark shadow colors from one side and light colors from the opposite side. This produces the desired illusion of three-dimensional form. The same effect can be achieved even if the light colors are eliminated entirely, as we have already seen in the example of the single color print (Fig. 41, Chapter 2). Using the glazing techniques described several paragraphs back, such a print, made on clear plastic, can be transformed into a transparency. The best results are obtained when the glazing is done on the paint side of the print.

Transparencies done in this manner have the brilliance of stained glass combined with the three-dimensionality of shaded form. They are most interesting when viewed against a window or some other light source. Unusual effects occur when two or more of these prints are superimposed over one another.

A representative sampling of designs can be found in the remaining pages of this chapter. These examples are offered with the hope that they will suggest ideas, and be of interest, to those readers who have been tempted to try their hands at relief transfer work.

80 Montage offset print on canvas made from an applicator stick relief.

82 Crisscrossing strips of construction paper formed the relief for this print.

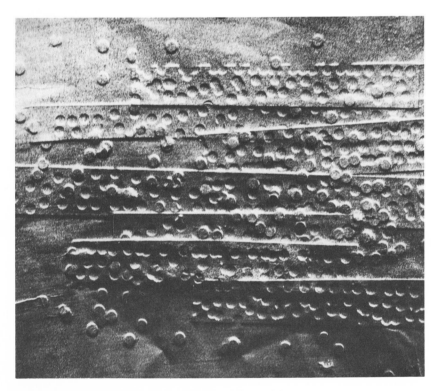

81 A hole puncher was used to make the relief for this print.

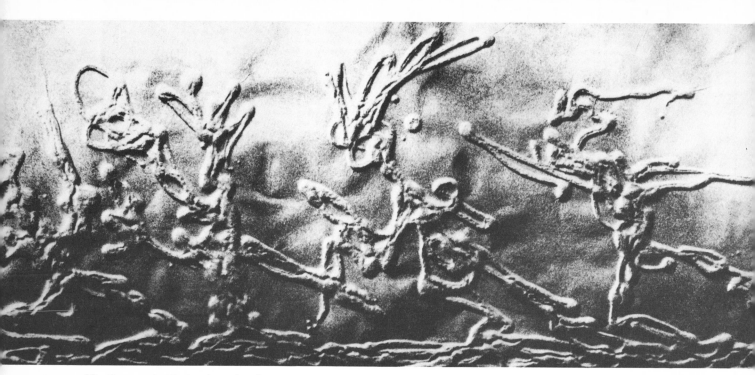

83 Squeeze-bottle drawing printed on acetate.

84 Montage design made from a modeling paste relief.

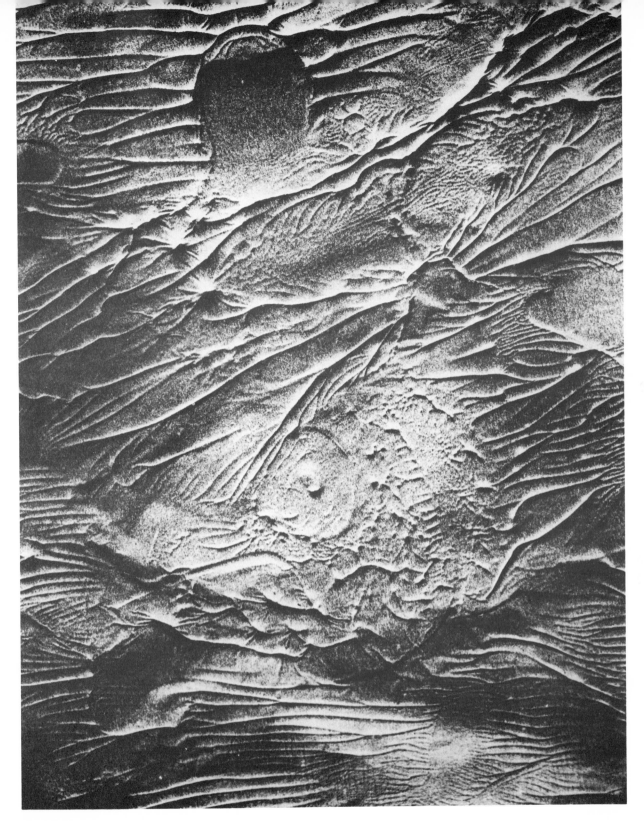

85 The relief surface for this print was made by spreading
gel on a board, pressing a piece of paper over it, then
peeling away the paper.

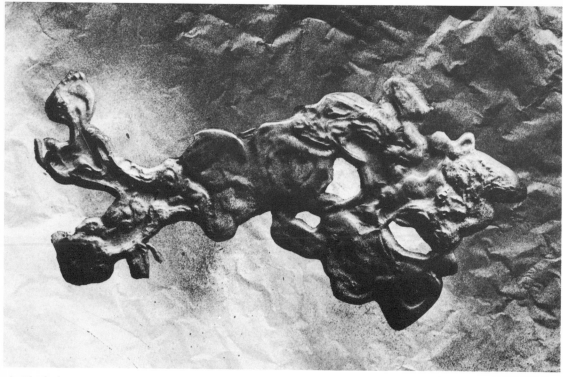

86 Squeeze-bottle design.

88 Spacescape. Another example of the cutout method.

87 Many different relief surfaces were used for the various cutouts that form this montage design.

89 Cutouts mounted against a painted background. The landscape portions were made from crumpled foil; the figure is a collage made from old scraps of painted foil.

90　Making a wood-grain rubbing.

92　Another cut-paper rubbing.

91　A cut-paper design, and the rubbing made from it.

93　This rubbing was cut out and mounted on a prepared background.

chapter 4
additional transfer techniques

All transfer techniques are fascinating, possibly because they satisfy a deep-seated human compulsion to duplicate and copy things. Several traditional techniques are reviewed in this concluding chapter. They were selected not only because they are useful and interesting in themselves, but because they are all related in certain respects to the relief transfer process. Several of them—monoprinting, rubbing, and photo-transfer, in particular—are direct forebears of relief transfer.

Rubbing

This is perhaps the easiest and best known of all transfer techniques. Choose a surface which has a design or texture in shallow relief and place a sheet of smooth newsprint over it. Next, take a crayon, preferably black or some other dark color, and remove all the paper. Rub the crayon flat across the paper with a firm, downward pressure. A few strokes will make every detail of the surface appear on the newsprint. (Fig. 90.)

Paper can be cut or torn into any desired shapes, arranged either realistically or abstractly, covered with newsprint, and rubbed in the same way. In the finished rubbing, overlapping pieces of paper will appear to pass through one another as though they were transparent. (Fig. 91.)

Paper designs can be inked and printed as well as rubbed. For this purpose the paper should be stronger and thicker than ordinary drawing paper. Oak tag is excellent. The cut shapes should be glued down flat to a sheet of thin cardboard or oak tag, then inked with a brayer. (Fig. 94.) The print can be made by hand, with a rolling pin or the back of a spoon, if no press is available.

There is no limit to the variety of surfaces that can be used for both printing and rubbing. Experiment. Exciting results can be obtained from such materials as: wood-grain; bark; feathers; pieces of material; leaves; bits of string or thread.

94 Inking a cut-paper design.

95 An assortment of cut-paper designs which can be used both for printing and rubbing.

96, 97 Additional cut-paper prints.

Photo-transfers

Using ordinary black and white newspaper photographs, you can make extremely interesting transfers in the following way: take a piece of illustration board or smooth, heavy drawing paper such as Bristol board and give it a single thin coat of rubber cement. When the rubber cement is dry, place the newspaper photograph face down over it and blacken the back with a soft lead pencil. When this is completed, the newspaper can be peeled away, leaving a print of the photograph on the illustration board. (Fig. 98.)

98 While peeling the paper away, you can see the photograph and its transfer simultaneously. This mirror effect can be preserved by gluing down the newspaper at the point where the image is most interesting.

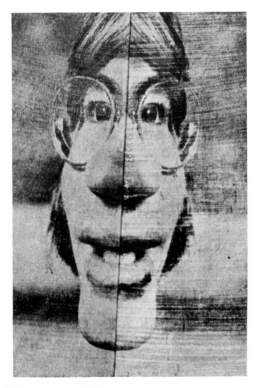

99 Mirror-image caricature.

100 Transfer of photograph of the singer Enrico Caruso.

101 A freely sketched photo-transfer.

102 Photographs can be cut up and glued to other photographs to create photo-collage transfers.

There are two reasons for using a pencil instead of a spoon or some other burnishing tool. First, by blackening the back of the photograph, you can always tell which areas have been done and which have not. Second, you can organize your pencil strokes into any desired pattern of lines, dots, or scribbles and this pattern will appear in the transferred photo. Transfers done this way often do not look like photographs at all, but like freely drawn, realistic pencil sketches. (Fig. 100.)

In general, these photo-transfers have a distinctive, slightly faded looking charm that is reminiscent of old daguerreotypes. Best results are obtained by using clear photographs with strong dark and light contrasts. If greater clarity is desired, the newspaper photograph can be touched up with pencil before the transfer is made; details such as hair texture can be sharpened or added, a shadow can be emphasized, or a shape can be changed. All of these penciled-in lines and shadings will transfer to the illustration board along with the photograph. (Fig. 102.)

103, 104 Two touched-up photo-transfers.

105 A scribbled transfer.

Color photo-transfers

Glossy magazine and newspaper photos, whether in color or black and white, cannot usually be transferred by the method just described. There is another way, however, to accomplish this with perfect accuracy. It is similar to the decalcomania method described in Chapter 2. Start by selecting a colored photograph from a magazine or newspaper. Brush a thick coat of polymer gel as evenly as possible over the entire picture. Set it aside and allow it to dry thoroughly overnight. While wet, gel is cloudy white in appearance, somewhat like skimmed milk, neither completely transparent nor completely opaque. When dry, it is perfectly clear and transparent. If there is no evidence of cloudiness, you will know that the gel coat is dry; you should then apply a second coat, in the same way, and allow it to dry overnight again.

When this second coat is dry, place the photo face down on a table and wet the back thoroughly using warm water and a wide brush. In a moment the paper will become soft and you can start rubbing it off with your fingers. Keep wetting the paper as you work being careful not to tear the gel skin; the photograph will remain printed on this skin after all of the paper has been rubbed off. (Fig. 106.)

If milky spots should appear on the gel when you wet it, don't worry; they will disappear gradually as the gel dries. When it is completely dry and clear again, it will be a transparent photograph printed on a transparent skin. (Fig. 107.)

Gel skin is fairly pliable at normal room temperature, but when it is held close to a hot radiator, or some other heat source, it becomes even more pliable and can be stretched, with care, like a sheet of rubber. Interesting distortions occur this way and

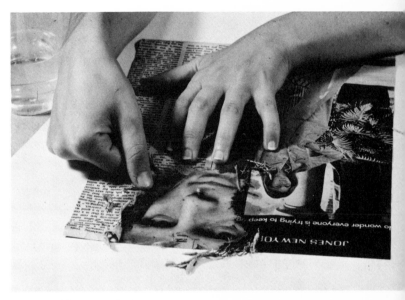

106 Rubbing away the wet paper.

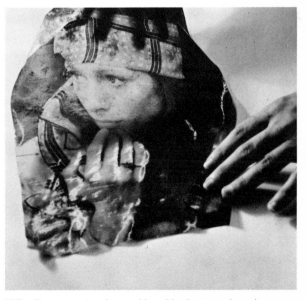

107 Transparent polymer skin with photograph on it.

can be preserved by mounting in the following manner: take a sheet of illustration board and coat it with rubber cement. Also coat the back of the polymer skin with rubber cement. Dry rubber cement surfaces stick to one another readily; therefore, when both coats are dry, the skin can be mounted simply by pressing it against the illustration board. While doing this, you can gently stretch the skin out of shape and cement it down before it has time to shrink back to normal. (Fig. 108.)

When the mounting is complete, remove all rubber cement remaining on any uncovered parts of the illustration board and cover the entire surface with a piece of transparent Con-Tact. This will serve to protect the picture and hold it in place so that it won't overcome the rubber cement and pull back to its original shape.

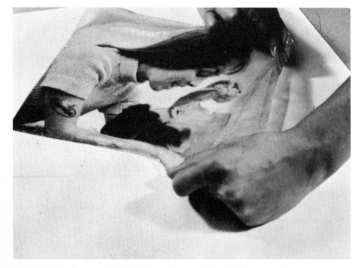

108 Stretching the polymer skin while mounting it.

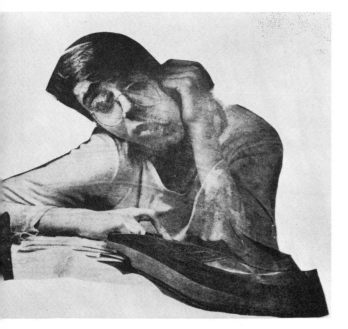

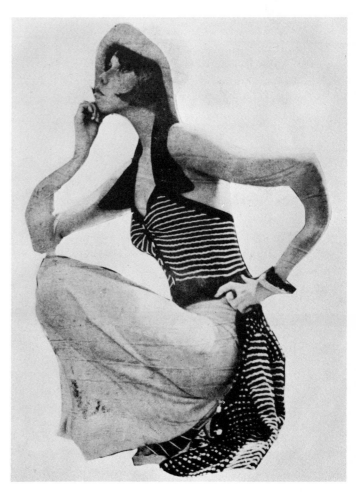

109-111 Examples of stretched polymer photos.

113 Examples of potato designs.

112 Making a potato-transfer.

Planographic potato-transfers

The most familiar type of transfer that is made with
a potato is the relief print: the potato is first sliced in
half, then linoleum cutting tools are used to carve
an incised design on the smooth, flat surface. Ink or
water color can then be applied to all of the raised
portions of the surface and a print can be made.

The planographic method, as its name indicates,
involves nothing but the flat surface. It requires no
carving tools of any kind other than a knife with
which to cut the potato in half. The procedure is as
follows: after cutting the potato in half, take one
of the halves and make the surface as flat and
smooth as possible by rubbing it over a piece of
coarse paper, such as manila, coarse newsprint, or
bogus paper. It should then be trimmed into a neat
rectangle.

Next, using a good pointed brush, paint a design

on the flat surface of the potato. Use ordinary paint
box colors. The paint should not be watery; it should
be drier and denser than when it is used on paper.
The naturally moist surface of the potato will compensate for the dryness of the paint and enable it
to flow from the brush easily. The finished design
can then be printed on any kind of absorbent printing or drawing paper. (Fig. 112.)

After making the print, you will notice that the
design has remained an indelible tattoo on the potato. Using the tattoo as a guide, you can repaint the
design and make a second print. This process can
be repeated as often as desired; the tattoo remains
indefinitely, guaranteeing that each paint applica-
tion will be the same as the preceding one. When
you no longer need that particular design, slice it
off, and you will have a clean surface to work on.

Stenciling

Stenciling is a method of transferring the shape of an object. If you were to pin a leaf to a piece of white paper and spray over it with black paint, the leaf could then be removed and its shape would remain, a white silhouette against a black background.

The simplest way to stencil is to cut out paper shapes, arrange them against a background, and spray with a color that contrasts strongly with that background. Canned spray paints are the easiest to use, but they can be unpleasant, and sometimes dangerous in crowded rooms that have poor air circulation. The most satisfactory way to spray is to use ordinary tempera colors that can be thinned with water. These paints can be mixed to produce any desired number of hues, tints, and shades. They can then be put into inexpensive hand-pumped insecticide sprayers such as the old-fashioned Flit gun. Results obtained this way are quite satisfactory.

Designs of any desired complexity can be created by shifting stencils around. Exciting rhythms are often the result, together with strange illusions of light and unexpected shapes arising from the overlapping of silhouettes. (Fig. 114.)

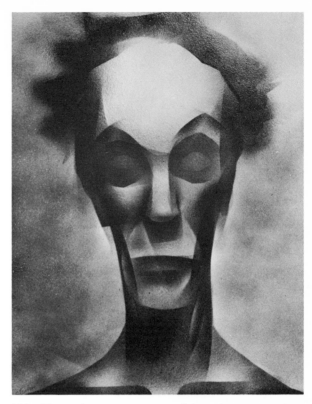

114 Pieces of cut paper, some straight and some curved, were the stencils for this portrait.

115 Scraps of torn paper were used to make this landscape.

116 A study in luminosity done with cut paper.

117 Illusion of three-dimensional form.

Three-dimensional effects can be achieved as follows: spray a piece of paper in such a way that you produce areas of dark and light blending into one another. Next, take a stencil—a circle, for example—and pin it over the paper so that part of it covers the dark background, and part of it covers the light background. Spray dark color around the edge of the stencil covering the light background, and spray light color around the edge of the stencil covering the dark background. When the stencil is removed, the remaining shape will have the solid appearance of a sphere floating in space (Fig. 117).

Almost anything can serve as a stencil—keys, washers, insects, dry cereal, different types of grain —the list is endless. One particularly interesting stencil deserves special attention—the painted stencil. Figure 118 is an example. First, background colors were sprayed over a sheet of paper. Next, a liquid latex compound was used to paint a stencil over this background. When the latex was dry, colors that contrasted with the background were sprayed over the entire design. When this paint was dry, the latex stencil was peeled away leaving its distinctive silhouette behind.

Three latex compounds that work extremely well are Miskit, Maskoid, and "Rubba-mold". There are undoubtedly many other similar, and equally effective, materials on the market. It should be pointed out that most of these latex compounds are water-based and should not be used on paper that is very absorbent. Illustration board, oak tag, and Bristol board give good results, and so do most water color papers.

118 This particular latex stencil design was done on scratchboard. When the spraying was finished, the paint dry, and all of the latex removed, lines were drawn in with a scratch-pen to add qualities of light and texture.

119 Four sandwich designs done with oil paint.

Sandwich designs

To make one of these unusual and colorful designs, do the following: take a piece of illustration board, or sturdy drawing paper, and coat it with spray-mounting adhesive. Squeeze small blobs of paint in a compact group anywhere on the paper, but not too near the edge. The blobs of paint should be touching one another; they can even be on top of one another. Next, take a thin sheet of clear acetate and press it down flat over everything. This will squash down the paint and cause it to spread slightly. With a brayer, or a rolling pin, spread the paint further. Finally, using a straight-edged piece of strong cardboard, squeegee the paint still more. This will cause it to mix in unexpected ways, producing extraordinary shapes, textures, and color combinations. At the same time, the acetate will glue itself to the spray adhesive wherever there is no paint. The result is an elegant, ''glassed-in'' design.

Actually, a sandwich design is a monoprint, transferred from the paper to the underside of the acetate. The making of the design and its transfer take place simultaneously. The most interesting effects are achieved with oil paints or acrylics. Tempera can also be used.

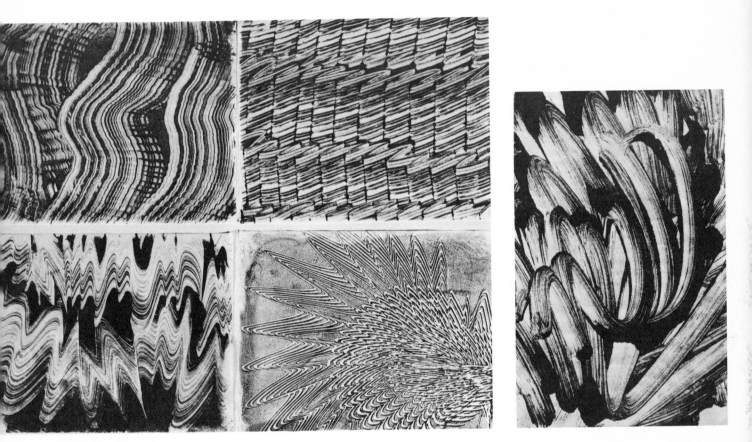

120, 121 Monoprints.

Monoprints

A monoprint is usually made by painting a design on a re-usable surface, such as glass or metal, and then printing it on another surface, usually paper. Once the design is transferred, the surface from which it was removed is ready for the next design.

Plate glass is excellent for monoprinting. Almost any kind of paint can be used. Oil paint thinned with turpentine is especially good. If you wish to use tempera, acrylics, or other water-based paints, you should brush a soap solution over the glass beforehand, otherwise the paint will not stick.

The procedure is quite simple. Make your painting on the glass with brushes, fingers, or whatever tools are desired. The paint should be neither too dry nor too wet, a requirement that can be met only through trial and error. When the painting is finished, place a sheet of absorbent paper over it. Pat and smooth it. When you lift up the paper, the design will come with it.

Each tool leaves its own distinctive mark, a transfer effect in its own right which can be noted in all the monoprints shown here. This effect, incidentally, can be demonstrated in drawing. If the drawing tool happens to be a notched crayon, for example, it will transfer to paper the distinctive characteristics that can be seen in Figures 122 and 123. A piece of notched cardboard can be used to create a similar effect with paint, as shown in Figure 124.

122 Drawing with a notched crayon.

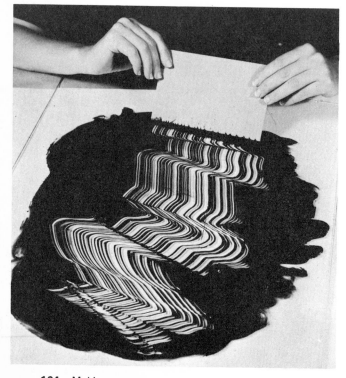

124 Making a monoprint with notched cardboard.

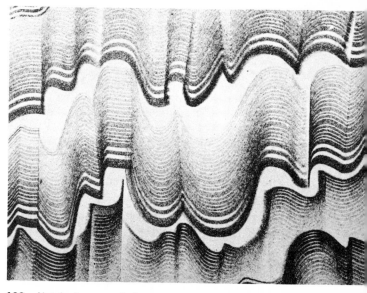

123 Notched crayon design.

125 A transparent fingerpainting.

126, 127 Additional transparencies.

Transparencies

One discovery always leads to another in art and sometimes the new discovery doesn't seem to bear much relationship to the one that led into it. This is true of the following technique, which has nothing to do with transfer designs but simply continues with the use of the notched cardboard previously mentioned. If for no other reason, it earns inclusion in this section by virtue of the excellent results it produces. It is a method of making transparencies with black paint on acetate.

Start by putting a thin, but solid, opaque coat of black acrylic paint over a sheet of clear acetate. The paint should be mixed with a little gel to help it stick to the acetate. Next, using a notched piece of cardboard as with the monoprints, make your design. Wherever the cardboard is applied, paint is removed and the clear acetate is exposed. When the paint is dry, transparent colors, such as lacquer stain, thinned oil paints, etc., can be painted over the clear areas. The design can then be placed against a window to produce a glowing stained-glass effect. Another approach, instead of painting the acetate with transparent colors, would be to simply mount the design against a multicolored background of some kind. White paper or crinkled foil, that has been sprayed with fluorescent colors, makes an excellent background.

Try fingerpainting with the black acrylic paint and gel mixture directly on acetate. The finished design can then either be mounted against a colored background, or stained with transparent colors and set against a window. Either way, the result will be quite brilliant. (Fig. 125.)

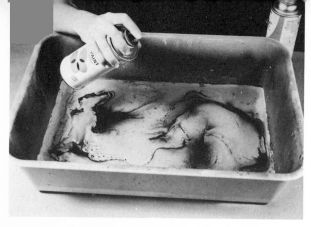

128 Spraying paint into the water.

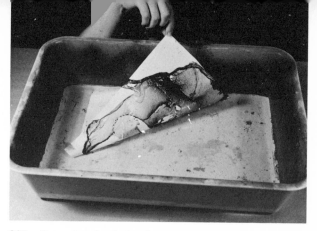

129 Removing the design from the water.

130 Floating transfer made with turpentine-thinned oil paint.

131 A collage combination.

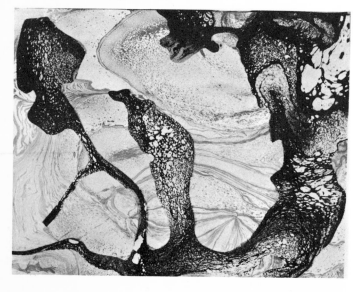

Floating transfers

This final transfer technique is, for many people, the most interesting of all. Results are always fascinating and no two designs are ever alike. Start by filling a large baking pan half full of water. The pan should be at least three inches deep and large enough to accommodate a sheet of paper 9″ x 12″ or larger. A circular pan is best because it enables the water to sustain its motion longer and more smoothly after it has been stirred. However, the conventional rectangular type is quite satisfactory.

Use quick-drying spray enamels. Spray successive colors directly into the water or against a sheet of paper held vertically over the surface of the water so that the paint will accumulate and drip into the water. The colors will immediately spread over the surface of the water, mixing with one another and creating striking effects of form and texture. This design can then be captured by dropping a flat sheet of paper onto the surface of the water, then carefully removing it. (Figs. 128 and 129.)

Differences in the physical properties of the various paints will cause them to behave differently on the water. Some will break up into beautiful, grainy textures, while others will spread smoothly and take on even-toned, biomorphic shapes.

Don't wait more than a few seconds before dropping the paper over the floating design. Spray paints dry almost instantly on the surface of the water, forming a dry, crinkly skin that is sometimes difficult to pick up. Best results are obtained while the paint is still wet.

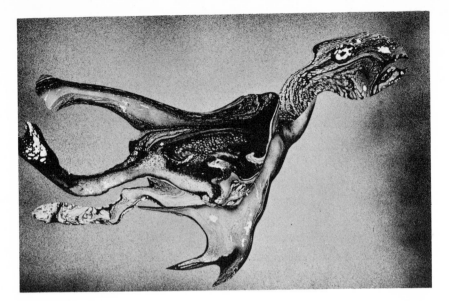

132 Hidden image.

If spray paints should prove to be impractical or undesirable, use regular tube oil paint thinned out with turpentine. The paint should be thin enough to drip off the end of a stick or brush, but not so thin that it has lost all of its color strength. When this paint is dripped into the water, it will spread and mix with other colors to provide exciting designs that are similar to those made with spray enamels. These designs can even be controlled to some extent by gently stirring the colors before dropping the paper over them.

Floating transfer designs can be used in many different ways: you can cut them up and rearrange them into collages, either abstract or representational (Fig. 131); you can search them for hidden images and discover chimera-like faces, plant forms, human and animal figures, all of which become startlingly real when they are cut out and mounted (Fig. 132); you can use them as backgrounds over which to paint, or mount cutouts and photographs (Fig. 133); and lastly, since they are so interesting to look at just as they are, you can simply frame them and hang them on your wall. Whichever way they are used, they are a never-ending source of fantasy and delight.

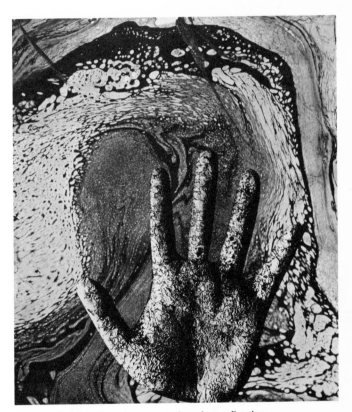

133 Relief transfer print mounted against a floating transfer background.

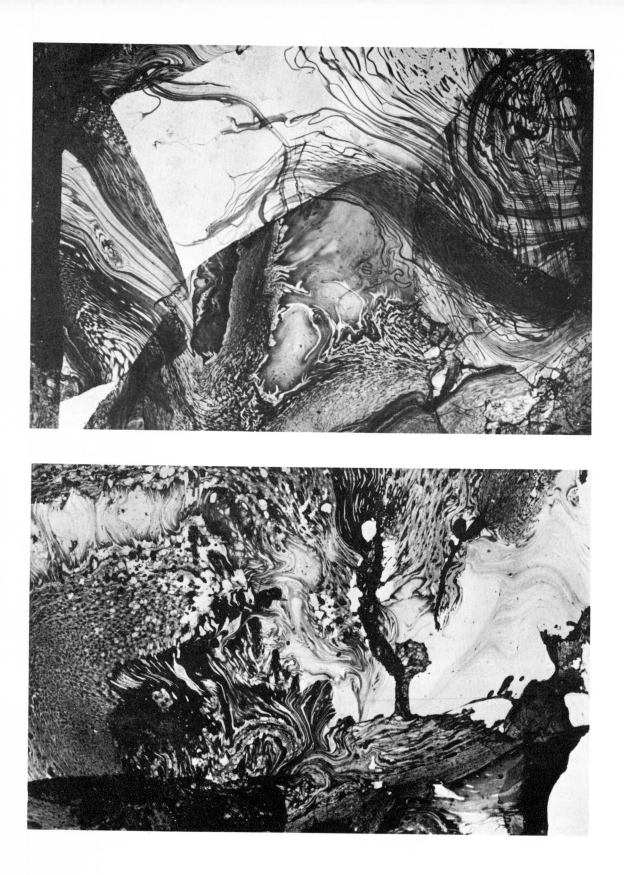

134-136 Additional examples of floating transfers.

postscript

I first began to experiment with my relief transfer process six years ago. Since then I have been continuously changing and refining it, and, at each stage, excitedly rediscovering its ready applicability to new ideas and materials. It is now developed to a point where it can be used effectively by artist and artist-teacher alike.

Many of its possibilities remain to be investigated, however, particularly in the area of design. A few likely applications immediately come to mind: floor and wall decorations; wrapping papers and parchments; designs for plastics, fabrics, wood, and metal. The technique, itself, can be extended to employ more sophisticated tools and materials than those that have been considered so far.

Obviously, there is still much to be discovered in the relief transfer process. It is new territory, waiting to be explored by those who never tire of searching out the wonders of light, shadow, and color.

H. S.

relief transfer materials and where to buy them

Acetate
This plastic can be bought by the sheet at most art supply and craft stores. Its thickness is measured in "points"—7 point, 10 point, and so on. 10 point clear acetate, which is approximately 1/64 of an inch thick, is fine for relief transfer printing.

Aluminum foil
Can be found in any supermarket.

Applicator sticks
Sold in drug stores; occasionally in craft stores.

Balsa wood
Sold in art supply and craft stores.

Bristol board
This excellent, heavy drawing paper is sold in art supply stores.

Canvas
Both primed (gesso coated) and unprimed canvas can be found in art supply and craft stores.

Construction paper
Comes in a variety of colors and can be purchased at art supply stores, craft stores, dime stores, and stationery stores.

Con-Tact One of several varieties of self-adhesive wall covering. The transparent type is the kind that is used for the projects described in this book. See Chapter 2.

Available in hardware stores, house furnishing stores, and paint stores.

Mounting boards
For mounting finished prints, matt board is best. However, illustration board and chipboard (heavy cardboard) can also be used. All of these can be found in art supply shops.

Paper trimmer
Excellent for cropping unwanted edges. Can be purchased at art supply and handicraft stores; also photographic supply and office supply stores.

Plaster of Paris
Carried by all paint stores and most hardware stores.

Plexiglas
Comes in various thicknesses and can be found in art supply and handicraft stores, and in some lumberyards.

Polymer
Liquid gloss medium, gel, gesso, and modeling paste, are all sold in art supply stores.

Razor blades
Only single-edge blades should be used. They can be purchased inexpensively in art supply and craft stores, or in hardware stores.

Rolling pins
Sold in hardware and house furnishing stores.

Rubber cement
Can be found in art supply stores, hardware stores, craft stores, and stationery stores.

Spray paint
Can be found in all paint stores, and most art supply and craft stores.

Squeegee
If you don't like using a homemade cardboard one, you can buy a real rubber one in an auto supply store or a hardware store. Excellent for making wet polymer prints.

Tape
Masking tape and cellophane tape are obtainable in art supply stores, hardware stores, and stationery stores.

Tissue paper
Craft stores and art supply stores sell all varieties of tissue paper.